SO-AHJ-586

Searchlight
BOOKS™

Predators

Wolves
on the Hunt

Meg Marquardt

Lerner Publications ◆ Minneapolis

Content Consultant: Ryan Scott, Regional Supervisor, Region I, Wildlife Conservation, Alaska Department of Fish and Game

Lerner Publications Company
A division of Lerner Publishing Group, Inc.
241 First Avenue North
Minneapolis, MN 55401 USA

For reading levels and more information, look up this title at
www.lernerbooks.com.

Library of Congress Cataloging-in-Publication Data

The Cataloging-in-Publication Data for *Wolves on the Hunt* is on file at the Library of Congress.
ISBN 978-1-5124-3399-9 (lib. bdg.)
ISBN 978-1-5124-5614-1 (pbk.)
ISBN 978-1-5124-5085-9 (EB pdf)

Manufactured in the United States of America
1 — CG — 7/15/17

Contents

Chapter 1
ON THE HUNT . . . page 4

Chapter 2
AROUND THE WORLD . . . page 9

Chapter 3
STRONG AND SPEEDY . . . page 14

Chapter 4
HOW WOLVES BEHAVE . . . page 20

Wolf Fact File • 28
Glossary • 30
Learn More about Wolves • 31
Index • 32

ON THE HUNT

A pack of wolves runs silently through the woods. It is wintertime, and the snow is thick under their paws. The sun shines brightly off the snow. The wolf pack has been following a herd of elk for 3 miles (5 kilometers). The elk catch the wolves' scent and break into a run. The wolves race after the herd.

Wolves can follow prey for a long time. What is one animal they might hunt?

The pack has been watching for the weakest member of the herd. Finally, they find it. One elk is sick. It falls behind the herd as it struggles to keep pace with the other elk. The wolves spring into action. The lighter females race ahead. The males chase behind the elk. They are quick and run across the top of the snow. But the elk is much heavier. Its flat hooves crunch right through the surface, slowing it down.

An elk that cannot keep up with its herd may become a wolf's next prey.

WOLVES WORK TOGETHER TO SEPARATE AN ELK FROM ITS HERD.

▼

Capturing Prey

As the wolves close in, they have to be careful. The elk is bigger than they are. One good kick from an elk can seriously injure a wolf. The females dart and dash around the large animal. This confuses the elk and makes it fall farther back from the herd. When the elk is completely separated, the rest of the wolves attack.

Looking for the Perfect Prey

Wolves sometimes go after weak animals. They are easier to catch. A weak animal might be one that is sick. Or it could be one that is older or simply can't keep up with the group. Sometimes wolves target newborn animals that cannot run fast enough to get away. However, wolves also kill healthy adults. Wolves use conditions such as deep snow to slow big animals down.

Newborn animals are not able to defend themselves against wolves, making them easier prey than healthy adults.

The alpha male and female lead the charge, followed by their young. The youngest pups stay back, learning from afar. The pack overwhelms the elk. The wolves claw and bite the elk, bringing it down. The wolves each devour several pounds of meat. Now they will not have to eat for several days. The pups eat the prey that their parents and older siblings kill. They may return to the kill over several days. When the pack moves on from the kill, the hunt will begin again. It may take several days to find and kill more prey.

A wolf shows its dominance over another wolf while the pack feeds.

Chapter 2

AROUND THE WORLD

Wolves are found in the northern part of the world. They live in North America, Europe, Asia, and Northeastern Africa. The most common wolf is the gray wolf, or *Canis lupus*. But there are two other distinct species of wolves as well. They are red wolves, or *Canis rufus*, and Ethiopian wolves, or *Canis simensis*.

Red wolves have more red in their coats than gray wolves. What is the third wolf species?

Species and Subspecies

The red wolf lives in the southeastern part of the United States. It can be found in the swampy, marshy forests of North Carolina. Ethiopian wolves live in the afro-alpine area of Africa. This is a mountainous region where vegetation tends to be sparse and not very tall. For the most part, these wolves hunt across open, hilly plateaus.

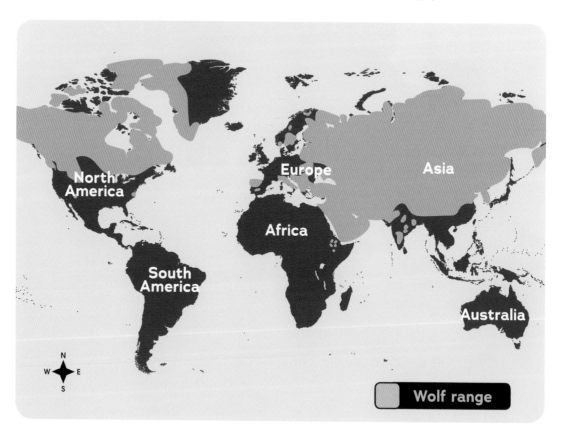

North America

Europe

Asia

Africa

South America

Australia

N
W   E
S

Wolf range

These gray wolves live in Europe.

As many as 74,100 gray wolves live in North America alone. They can be found mostly in the northern part of North America. Packs of gray wolves roam Alaska, Canada, and the Great Lakes region. There is also a special group of gray wolves that was reintroduced to Yellowstone National Park. The Yellowstone wolves were introduced into the park to save the species from population loss in other regions.

Wolves tend to live in remote places. They are very territorial, meaning they try to keep other wolf competitors from their hunting grounds. Some gray wolves live in Canada's dense woods or in the snowy regions around the Rocky Mountains.

Some wolves, such as this Ethiopian wolf, live in mountainous areas.

Many wolves are subspecies of the gray wolf. This means they are separated by geography. They may look and behave slightly differently from other subspecies, but they are capable of breeding with the other subspecies. One subspecies, the Arctic wolf, lives in northern Canada, Alaska, and Greenland. Another subspecies, the Iberian wolf, lives in Spain and Portugal.

Wolves can be found in all sorts of climates. They live in places with temperatures that range from -70 to 120°F (-57 to 49°C), though they generally live in less extreme places. To live in such varied conditions, they must be masters of adaptation.

Wolf or Fox?

A long-legged, red-furred animal lives in the forests of South America. It is known as the maned wolf. However, this creature is not really a wolf. Its red coloring and huge ears make it look more like a fox. Yet it is not a fox either. The maned wolf is a unique species. It is the only member of the genus *Chrysocyon*, meaning "golden dog."

The maned wolf is named for the dark mane that grows on the back of its neck.

Chapter 3

STRONG AND SPEEDY

Wolves come in many shapes and sizes. Gray wolves grow to be around 4.5 to 6.5 feet (1.4 to 2 meters) long and weigh about 50 to 130 pounds (23 to 59 kilograms). That is about as heavy as one to two dishwashers. They are various shades of gray, black, and white. The Ethiopian wolf is much smaller, weighing from 24 to 42 pounds (11 to 19 kg). Its fur tends to be a brownish-gold.

The same pack of gray wolves can be a wide variety of colors. What colors make up their coats?

Wolves that live in different regions have different adaptations. For example, Arctic wolves have snowy-white coats that hide them in the snow. Red wolves, on the other hand, live in the woods of North Carolina. They have thin, reddish coats that help them blend in with their surroundings. Since North Carolina is warmer than the Arctic, they do not need a very thick coat.

Arctic wolves' shorter ears and muzzles keep them warmer in cold climates because there is less surface area for body heat to escape.

Senses

Some adaptations are true of all wolves. Wolves have excellent hearing. In the woods, they can hear up to 6 miles (9.7 km) away. On a wide-open plain, they can hear up to 10 miles (16 km). Wolves have also adapted a keen nose. They can smell prey at a distance of up to 1.75 miles (2.82 km) away.

WOLVES ALSO USE THEIR NOSES TO FIND OUT IF THERE ARE OTHER PACKS NEARBY.

Saving Red Wolves

In the mid-1900s, territory loss caused red wolf populations to drop, as did human overhunting of deer, the wolves' main prey. By 1980, the last wild wolves were taken into captivity. However, direct intervention by breeding programs has brought the wolves back. Programs bred some of the captive wolves and released their offspring. In 2013, around one hundred red wolves roamed free in North Carolina. Nearly two hundred are still in captivity for breeding.

Captive breeding saved the red wolf from extinction.

Wolves use their strong jaws to bite through bone.

Going In for the Kill

Wolves use their strong jaws to clamp onto prey. The pressure of their bite is up to 1,500 pounds per square inch (1,034 newtons per square centimeter). Humans can manage only 300 pounds per square inch (207 N per sq. cm). A wolf's bite can crush the bones of smaller prey. Bones have protein in the middle called bone marrow. By biting into bones and eating the marrow, wolves can get more nutrients such as protein.

Wolves have several important adaptations for hunting. One is speed. A wolf can run up to 35 miles (56 km) per hour. Their feet are also adapted to running in snowy climates. Because wolf paws spread out as they hit the ground, they work like snowshoes. The wolf can run on the snow's surface without cracking through the top. And wolves' stomachs can handle up to 20 pounds (9 kg) of meat at one time.

Wolves' speed helps them outmaneuver larger prey.

Chapter 4

HOW WOLVES BEHAVE

Wolves are pack animals. Their packs can be as small as just two members, one male and one female. However, the pack is often larger. The pack may include offspring of the alpha male and female, the most dominant members of the pack. Other pack members may have joined from another pack, though this is rare. Typically, packs are around 10 to 15 members.

Wolf packs hunt and rest together. How many wolves are usually in a pack?

Body language can show dominance (*left*) or submission (*right*) or communicate other things to the pack.

Wolves communicate with one another using a range of different noises. They may bark or growl in warning. But what they are best known for is howling. Their howls are loud and carry across long distances. Wolves howl to bring their pack together when members are separated. They also howl to warn other wolves off their territory.

Guarding territory is an important part of wolf behavior. Their territories can range in size from 50 to 1,000 square miles (129 to 2,590 square kilometers). The size of the range depends on how much prey is available. If prey is scarce, wolves may claim a large range. Wolf territories can also change based on new packs forming nearby or human land use. Wolves mark their territory primarily with scent. They leave urine or feces at the edges of their territories. That warns other wolves that they are entering a claimed territory that the pack will defend.

Wolves in areas with fewer prey have larger territories than wolves in areas with a lot of prey.

Knowing the Territory

Wolves are observant of their prey and the environment. Big, hooved animals such as moose or caribou can run faster, especially in wide-open fields. But wolves use their environment to their advantage. Wolves may stalk their prey in wooded areas. Or they may try to force prey onto uneven ground, such as a dry riverbed or dried-up lake. Big, round stones in these areas can make it hard for animals with hooves to walk. Agile wolves can then take them down.

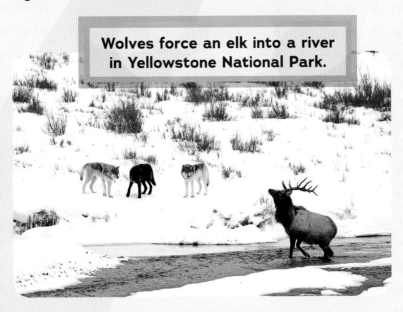

Wolves force an elk into a river in Yellowstone National Park.

Growing Up

Young wolves are often the pack's focus. Usually only the alpha male and female of the group breed. They typically mate for life. Wolves mate in winter. Females give birth in April or May. A litter may have four to six pups. During their first few weeks, wolf pups are almost defenseless. They are born completely blind and deaf. They rely on their mother for everything, including food. For the first three weeks, pups might feed four to six times a day.

Newborn pups cannot see or hear when they are born.

At first, pups stay close to their mother while exploring.

By three weeks, though, the pups start exploring outside the den. At five weeks, they start eating meat that their mother or other wolves have eaten and regurgitated, or brought back up from their stomachs. Eventually, though, they begin eating fresh meat. During the fall and winter months, they watch the way their parents and older siblings take down prey.

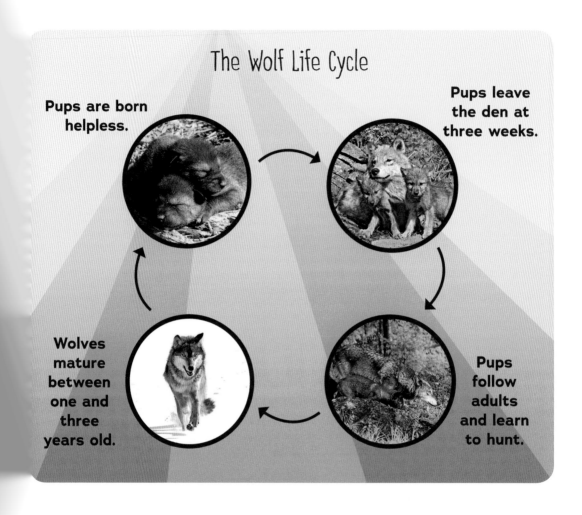

The Wolf Life Cycle

Pups are born helpless.

Pups leave the den at three weeks.

Wolves mature between one and three years old.

Pups follow adults and learn to hunt.

By their first winter, young wolves are ready to join the hunt. When they are one to three years old, they may join another pack. Wolves often leave a pack due to competition over breeding or food resources. Some even start their own pack, marking out all new territory.

Wolves are often the apex, or top, predators in their region. Their senses and stamina let them track prey for miles. Their teamwork lets them take down large prey. Since they focus on weak prey, their hunting strengthens the prey populations in their range. As long as wolves are on the move, they are on the hunt.

Wolves can travel more than 50 miles (80 km) a day to find food.

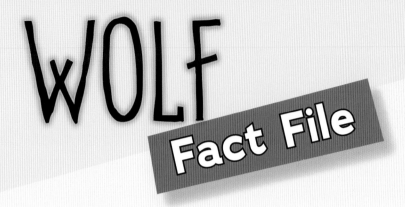

WOLF
Fact File

Scientific Name: *Canis lupus, Canis rufus, Canis simensis*

Where It Is Found: the northern part of the globe, primarily North America, Europe, northern Africa, and Asia

Habitat: woods, mountains, grasslands, tundra

Diet: deer, caribou, moose, rodents, lizards

Height: 21 to 32 inches (53–81 cm) at the shoulder

Length: 4.5 to 6.5 feet (1.4–2 m) (gray wolf)

Weight: 24 to 130 pounds (11–59 kg)

Life Span: 5 to 12 years in the wild

Food Chain

Glossary

adaptation: changes in living things that make them better able to survive in an environment

afro-alpine: a region of Africa that is mountainous and has grassland vegetation

agile: able to move and turn quickly and gracefully

caribou: large, hooved animals that live in northern North America

climate: the weather of a certain place during a period of time

feces: animal waste, or poop

litter: a group of baby wolves

marrow: soft tissue inside of bones

plateau: a flat piece of land in a hilly or mountainous region

subspecies: a member of a species that lives in a particular geographic region and may look or behave a bit differently from other subspecies but is capable of mating with other subspecies

territory: a defended area of land

Learn More about Wolves

Books

Brandenburg, Jim, and Judy Brandenburg. *Face to Face with Wolves*. Washington, DC: National Geographic, 2010. Learn how wolves hunt across a range of habitats, seeking to be the top predator of each.

Jazynka, Kitson, and Daniel Raven-Ellison. *Mission: Wolf Rescue*. Washington, DC: National Geographic Kids, 2014. Find out how people can save wolves from possible extinction.

Simon, Charnan. *Wolves*. Danbury, CT: Children's Press, 2012. Explore wolves' hunting strategies and how wolves are similar to domestic dogs.

Websites

African Wildlife Foundation: Ethiopian Wolf
http://www.awf.org/wildlife-conservation/ethiopian-wolf
Read about the challenges Ethiopian wolves face and explore photos of the species.

International Wolf Center: Wild Kids
http://www.wolf.org/wolf-info/wild-kids
Fun facts, activities, and games cover all there is to know about wolves.

***National Geographic Kids*: Gray Wolf**
http://kids.nationalgeographic.com/animals/gray-wolf/#gray-wolf-closeup.jpg
Discover amazing facts about wolves and other animals that live in wolf territories.

Index

adaptations, 15–16, 18–19

alphas, 8, 20, 24

communication, 21

elk, 4–6, 8
Ethiopian wolf, 9–10, 14

gray wolf, 9, 11–12, 14

habitat, 9–12, 15
hunting, 4–8, 10, 17, 19, 26–27

packs, 4–5, 8, 11, 20–22, 24, 26
prey, 6–8, 16–18, 22–23, 25, 27

red wolf, 9–10, 15, 17

senses, 16, 27
size, 14
subspecies, 12

territory, 11, 17, 21–22, 26

Yellowstone National Park, 11

Photo Acknowledgments

The images in this book are used with the permission of: © KenCanning/iStock.com, p. 4; © Kat72/ iStock.com, p. 5; © Donald M. Jones/Minden Pictures/Newscom, pp. 6, 23; © Richard Seeley/ Shutterstock.com, p. 7; © Carlyn Iverson/Science Source, p. 8; © jeanro/iStock.com, p. 9; © Red Line Editorial, p. 10; © s-eyerkaufer/iStock.com, p. 11; © AlbertoLoyo/iStock.com, p. 12; © anankkml/ iStock.com, p. 13; © Dennis W Donohue/Shutterstock.com, p. 14; © Cybernesco/iStock.com, p. 15; © gkuchera/iStock.com, p. 16; © Ryan Nordsven/USFWS, pp. 17, 24, 26 (top left); © Ken Conger/ National Park Service, p. 18; © Chris Stenger/Buiten-beeld/Minden Pictures/Newscom, p. 19; © Andyworks/iStock.com, p. 20; © outdoorsman/Shutterstock.com, p. 21; © milehightraveler/ iStock.com, p. 22; © JohnPitcher/iStock.com, pp. 25, 26 (top right); © hkuchera/iStock.com, pp. 26, (bottom left), 27; © Louise Heusinkveld/Oxford Scientific/Getty Images, p. 26 (bottom right); © JackF/iStock.com, p. 29 (top); © Drakuliren/iStock.com, p. 29 (middle left); © Sylvie Bouchard/ Shutterstock.com, p. 29 (middle right); © Roger Asbury/iStock.com, p. 29 (bottom).

Front Cover: © twildlife/iStock.com.

Main body text set in Adrianna Regular 14/20.
Typeface provided by Chank.